It's fun to draw
Safari
Animals

Mark Bergin

Author:
Mark Bergin was born in Hastings, England. He
has illustrated an award winning series and written
over twenty books. He has done many book
designs, layouts and storyboards in many styles
including cartoon for numerous books, posters and
adverts. He lives in Bexhill-on-sea with his wife
and three children.

Editorial Assistant:
Rob Walker

HOW TO USE THIS BOOK:

Start by following the numbered splats on the left
hand page. These steps will ask you to add some
lines to your drawing. The new lines are always
drawn in red so you can see how the drawing
builds from step to step. Read the 'You can do it!'
splats to learn about drawing and shading
techniques you can use.

Published in Great Britain in MMXI by
Book House, an imprint of
The Salariya Book Company Ltd
25 Marlborough Place, Brighton BN1 1UB
www.salariya.com
www.book-house.co.uk

ISBN-13: 978-1-906714-33-8

PAPER FROM
SUSTAINABLE
FORESTS

Visit our website at **www.book-house.co.uk**
or go to **www.salariya.com** for **free** electronic versions of:
You Wouldn't Want to be an Egyptian Mummy!
You Wouldn't Want to be a Roman Gladiator!
You Wouldn't Want to be a Polar Explorer!
You Wouldn't Want to Sail on a 19th-Century Whaling Ship!

Visit our Bookhouse 100 channel on Youtube to see Mark
Bergin doing step by step illustrations:

www.youtube.com/user/BookHouse100

Contents

Zebra

1 Start with the head and a dot for the eye.

2 Add ears, mouth, nostrils and hair.

3 Draw in the neck to a bean-shaped body.

you can do it!

Use wax crayons for background texture painted over with watercolour paint. Use black felt-tip for the zebra's stripes.

4 Add the mane and the tail.

splat-a-fact

No two zebra stripes are exactly the same.

5 Draw four legs and hooves.

4

Lion

1 Start with the head and add two dots for the eyes.

2 Add the nose, mouth and whiskers and draw in the mane.

3 Add the body with a curly tail and four legs with big paws.

you can do it!

Use wax crayons to colour and a felt-tip for the lines.

Splat-a-fact

Lions rest for about 20 hours each day.

6

Giraffe

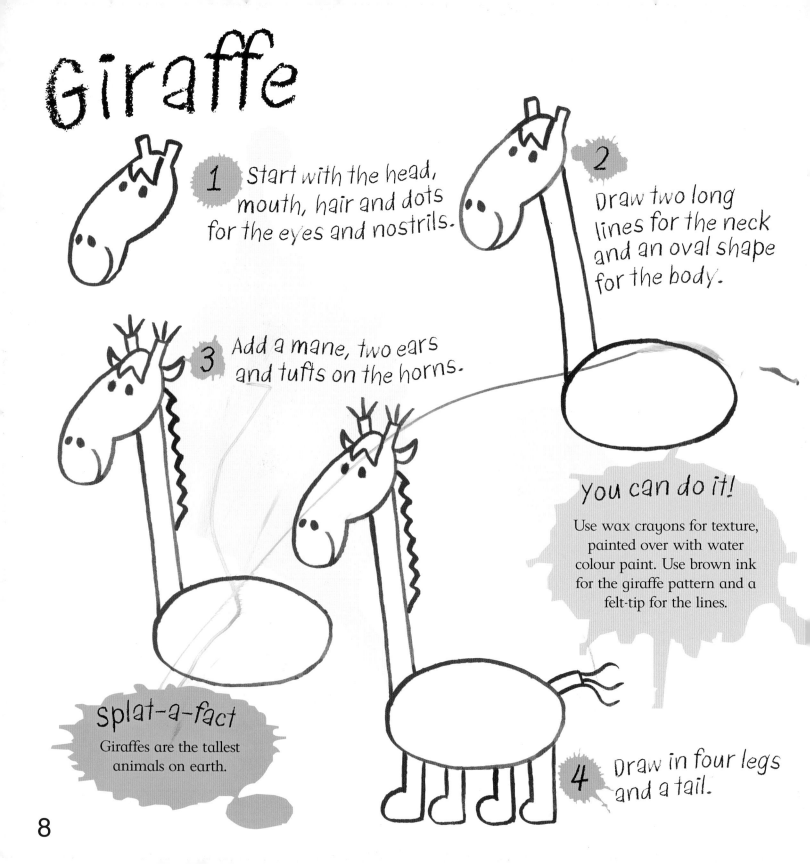

1 Start with the head, mouth, hair and dots for the eyes and nostrils.

2 Draw two long lines for the neck and an oval shape for the body.

3 Add a mane, two ears and tufts on the horns.

you can do it!

Use wax crayons for texture, painted over with water colour paint. Use brown ink for the giraffe pattern and a felt-tip for the lines.

splat-a-fact

Giraffes are the tallest animals on earth.

4 Draw in four legs and a tail.

Ostrich

1 Start with the head, adding a beak and a dot for the eye.

2 Draw two lines for the neck.

3 Draw an oval shape with a flat bottom for the body. Add a line at the front and the wing.

4 Add two legs with clawed feet and big tail feathers.

you can do it!
Use oil pastels, and use your finger to smudge them. Use a felt-tip for the lines.

10

Eagle

1 Start with the head and the body.

2 Add an eye, a beak, two feet and tail feathers.

3 Draw two wings.

you can do it!
Use wax crayons for the feather shapes and textures. Paint over with watercolour paint. Use a felt-tip for the lines.

splat-a-fact
Eagles have excellent eyesight and razor-sharp talons.

4 Add the wing feathers.

13

Wildebeest

1 Start with the head and the horns.

2 Add two ears and dots for the eyes and nostrils.

splat-a fact

A wildebeest is also called a gnu (noo).

you can do it!

Add colour with watercolour paint and use a sponge to dab more colour on for added texture. Use a felt-tip for the lines.

3 Draw the body shape and neck.

4 Add four legs and a tail.

Elephant

1 Start by cutting out the shape of the head.

2 Cut out the tusk and add a dot for an eye.

3 Cut an oval for the body.

splat-a-fact

An elephant is the only mammal that cannot jump.

MAKE SURE YOU GET AN ADULT TO HELP YOU WHEN USING SCISSORS!

4 Cut out the tip of the tail, four legs and draw in the toenails.

Leopard

you can do it!
Use coloured pencils and felt-tip for the lines.
Use both for the leopard's spots.

1 Start with the head.

2 Add ears, nose, mouth and a dot for an eye.

3 Draw in the neck and the body.

4 Add whiskers and a tail.

splat-a-fact
Leopards are great climbers and like to eat and sleep in trees.

5 Draw in four legs and paws.

18

Warthog

1 Start with the head and a dot for the eye.

2 Draw in neck, hair, tusks and ears.

Splat-a-fact

A warthog kneels on its front legs to eat.

3 Draw the body shape.

you can do it!

Use a dark pencil for the outline and add colour with watercolour paint.

4 Add four legs, a tail and two dots for nostrils.

20

Thomson's gazelle

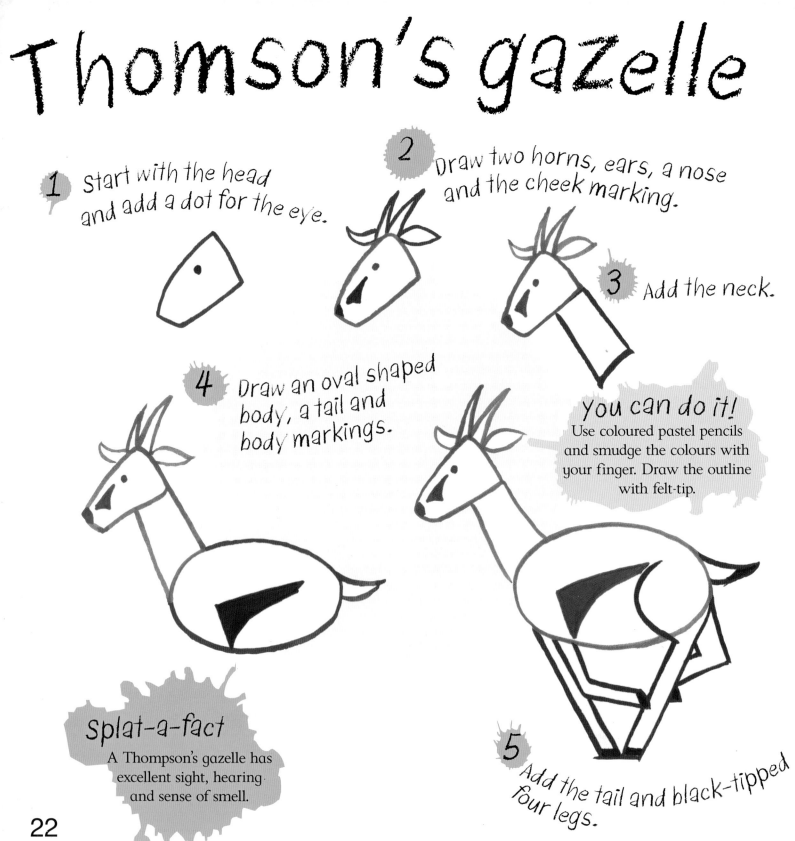

1 Start with the head and add a dot for the eye.

2 Draw two horns, ears, a nose and the cheek marking.

3 Add the neck.

4 Draw an oval shaped body, a tail and body markings.

you can do it!
Use coloured pastel pencils and smudge the colours with your finger. Draw the outline with felt-tip.

Splat-a-fact
A Thompson's gazelle has excellent sight, hearing and sense of smell.

5 Add the tail and black-tipped four legs.

Crocodile

1 Start with the head.

2 Add a nostril, eye, teeth and two small bumps.

3 Draw two lines for the body and tail and a line for its belly.

you can do it!
Use coloured inks and a felt-tip for the lines.

4 Add four legs, spikes on its back, lines across its belly and above the eye.

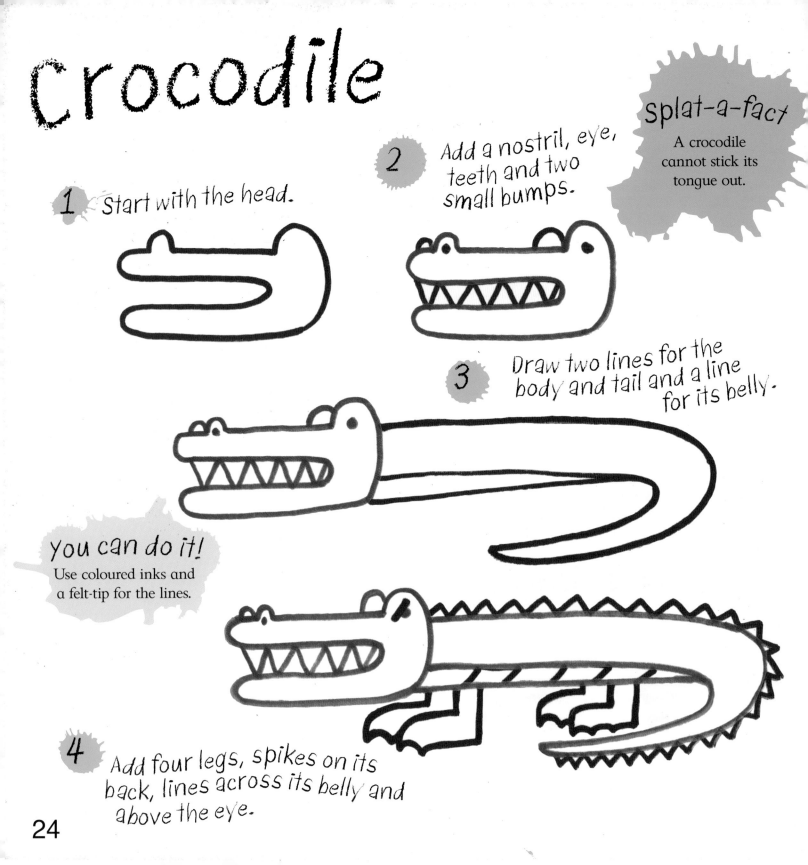

Baboon

A group of baboons is called a troop.

1 Start with the head and chest.

2 Add the body and lots of fur.

3 Draw in the tail, one ear and dots for eyes and nostrils.

you can do it!

Use wax crayons for texture and paint over it with watercolour paint. Use felt-tip for the lines.

4 Add two front legs and two back legs.

Hippo

1 Start with the head and two dots for the eyes.

2 Add two ears and a mouth.

3 Draw a big oval body.

4 Add a tail and four legs with toenails.

splat-a-fact
Hippos spend most of the day in water but they do not swim.

Cheetah

1 Start with a head.

2 Add a dot for the eye and the mouth.

3 Add a long oval shape for the body, two lines for the neck and a dot for the nose.

you can do it!

Draw the outlines in brown felt tip. Colour in with coloured pencils.

4 Add the tail.

5 Add four legs.

splat-a-fact

A cheetah can run as fast as a car - up to 75 miles per hour!

Index